Paper Gifts and Jewelry

•FLORENCE TEMKO•

The Millbrook Press
Brookfield, Connecticut

W9-AXZ-086

Published in the United States in 1997 by

The Millbrook Press, Inc.
2 Old New Milford Road
Brookfield, Connecticut 06804

First published in Great Britain in 1995 by

Dragon's World Limited
London House, Great Eastern Wharf
Parkgate Road, LONDON SW11 4NQ

© 1995 Dragon's World Limited
Text and paper project designs
  © 1995 Florence Temko

Text: Florence Temko
Editor: Kyla Barber
Design: Mel Raymond, Bob Scott
Illustrations: John Walls
Art Director: John Strange
Editorial Director: Pippa Rubinstein

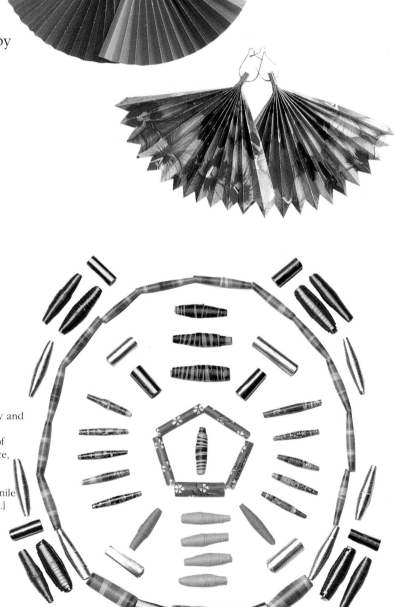

Library of Congress Cataloging-In-Publication Data
Temko, Florence.
  Paper gifts and jewelry / Florence Temko.
    p. cm. -- (Paper magic)
  British ed. published in 1995 under the title: Gifts, jewellery and
other ideas.
  Summary: Provides instructions for making an assortment of
jewelry and gifts from paper, including a paper bead necklace,
masks, window hangings, and a treasure box.
  ISBN 0-7613-0209-3 (lib. ed.).
  1. Paper work--Juvenile literature. 2. Jewelry making--Juvenile
literature. [1. Paper work. 2. Jewelry making. 3. Handicraft.]
I. Title. II. Series: Temko, Florence. Paper magic.
TT870.T46115 1997
745.54--dc20   96-28132
                                      CIP
                                      AC

CONTENTS

One, two, or three boxes next to a heading indicate the degree of difficulty.

Easy

You can do it

Take your time

INTRODUCTION

Everyone, including you, likes to receive a gift. This book shows how you can make jewelry and other gifts with ordinary paper or beautiful giftwrap.

Jewelry

It's fun to make your own jewelry because it's easy. You can take all kinds of colorful paper and turn it into earrings, bracelets, pins, headbands, and other body decorations.

Some of the jewelry can be finished in minutes while other pieces may be a real challenge. You can copy the designs exactly or change them in any way you like to suit your mood and to match your clothes. This book will show you how to create paper jewelry you'll be proud to wear and give away as presents and tokens of friendship.

Other gift ideas

Your friends and family will also be pleased to receive brightly colored mosaics and beautiful stained glass windows, specially designed and made for them.

You can wrap up your gifts in crayon wrapping paper that you have made yourself or you can put them in little decorative boxes.

To help you follow each step easily, the numbers next to the text match the corresponding drawings.

Measurements

All dimensions are given in inches and centimeters. They are not always exactly equal to avoid too many fractions. Either set will work well.

KEY TO SYMBOLS

Crease paper up (valley fold)

- - - - - - - - - - - - - - -

A crease made before

_____

Cut

_____ ✂

Arrow points in the direction in which the paper is to be folded

Double arrow means fold and then unfold the crease

Turn the paper over from back to front

ABOUT PAPER AND JEWELRY SUPPLIES

Almost any kind of paper can be turned into paper jewelry. At the beginning of each project you will find a listing of the paper and other materials you need.

Paper: Giftwrap, stationery, computer paper, printing paper, colored art paper, or metallic foil paper.

Stiff paper or thin cardboard: This is about the same stiffness and weight that you find in ready-made greeting cards. Choose cardboard, or card, construction paper, poster paper or posterboard, Bristol paper, Strathmore, index cards, or oaktag. Sharpen any creases by going over them with a ruler.

Reuse, recycle

Before you throw away any piece of paper, think about whether you could use it again. As you make the things shown in this book, you will be cutting up a lot of paper. You can easily recycle all those funny shapes that fall off. Turn them into stickers.

Glue

You can use your favorite glue, but always spread on as little as possible. Otherwise, the paper may buckle. My favorite glues are glue sticks (they must be fresh) and white glue. With certain types of glue sticks the paper may be lifted off again so that you can rearrange a design until you're satisfied with it.

Finishes

Jewelry made from paper is quite strong and can be worn many times. Many people believe paper jewelry should be covered with a finish to make it last longer. These are some of the methods you can use:

- Brush white glue on the jewelry. It will dry transparent, even if you repeat the process several times. Do not use white glue on metallic foil, however, as it will dull the foil. Other acrylic mediums work the same way.
- Clear nail polish.
- When you dip jewelry into plastic finishes they will end up hard as glass. These finishes are quite dangerous to handle and are not recommended, except under adult supervision.
- Clear self-adhesive plastic (Con-Tact or other brand) can be applied before making the jewelry or after it's finished.

Jewelry supplies

For some paper jewelry you need supplies, or findings, such as earring wires or clips or brooch backs. They are sold in craft and bead stores.

For earrings: You can hang earrings around your ears with loops of thread. Or you can buy metal earring loops for pierced ears or clips for unpierced ears.

For brooches and pins: Glue on a brooch back or attach a safety pin with strong sticky tape.

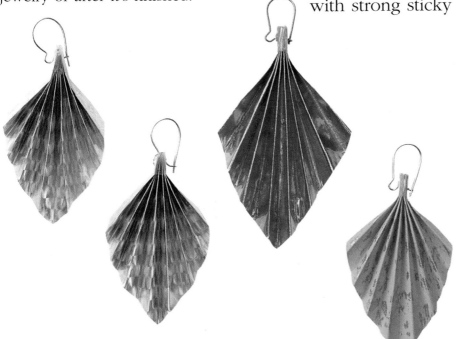

FAN EARRINGS AND BROOCH

These are the simplest earrings and brooch you can make. Fan pleat small pieces of paper and attach jewelry findings. If you don't have any, you can use loops of thread for the earrings or a safety pin for the brooch.

You will need
Giftwrap
Pencil, ruler, scissors
Thread and needle
or earring findings
(see page 7)

1 Cut two pieces of giftwrap 5 by 2 inches (12 by 5 centimeters). You can measure with a ruler.

2 Fan pleat the paper like this: Fold the paper in half; and fold it in half again. Unfold the paper flat. Pleat the paper up and down on the creases and in between.

3 Wind a narrow piece of sticky tape around one end of the closed fan. Spread open the other end. Thread the needle and push it through the closed end. You may want to ask an adult to help you.

Fan Brooch

Begin with a piece of paper larger than for the earrings. Follow the instructions for pleating. Place the fan on a piece of card. Draw around it. Cut the card smaller than the outline. Glue the fan on it by putting dabs of glue on the ridges of the fan. Glue a brooch back to the other side of the card. If you do not have a brooch back, attach a safety pin with strong tape.

Spiky edges

Close the fan and cut the bottom edge at an angle, a few pleats at a time.

Tip

If you are using fairly thick paper, it may be difficult to push the needle through for attaching the earring findings. Here is a trick: Before you tape the end in step 3, cut away a narrow strip at the top.

 Fan Earrings.

SHELL EARRINGS

Shell Earrings are pleated just like fans, but end up with beautiful curves. You can use giftwrap, magazine pages, origami or other colored papers, but with foil giftwrap, the earrings will sparkle like diamonds.

You will need
Giftwrap
Pencil, ruler, scissors
Tape
Thread and needle
or earring findings
(see page 7)

1 Cut two pieces of giftwrap 5 by 2 inches (12 by 5 centimeters). Each piece makes one earring. Fold the paper in half the short way.

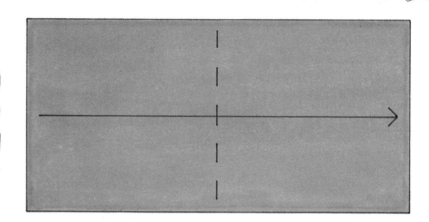

2 Draw a diagonal line beginning at the folded edge to the other side. Cut on the line.

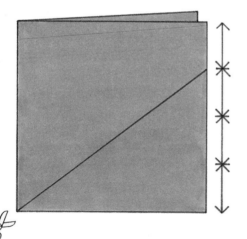

3 Fan pleat the paper like this: Fold the paper in half; and fold it in half again. Unfold the paper flat. Pleat the paper up and down on the creases and in between.

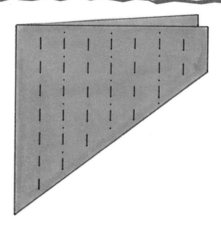

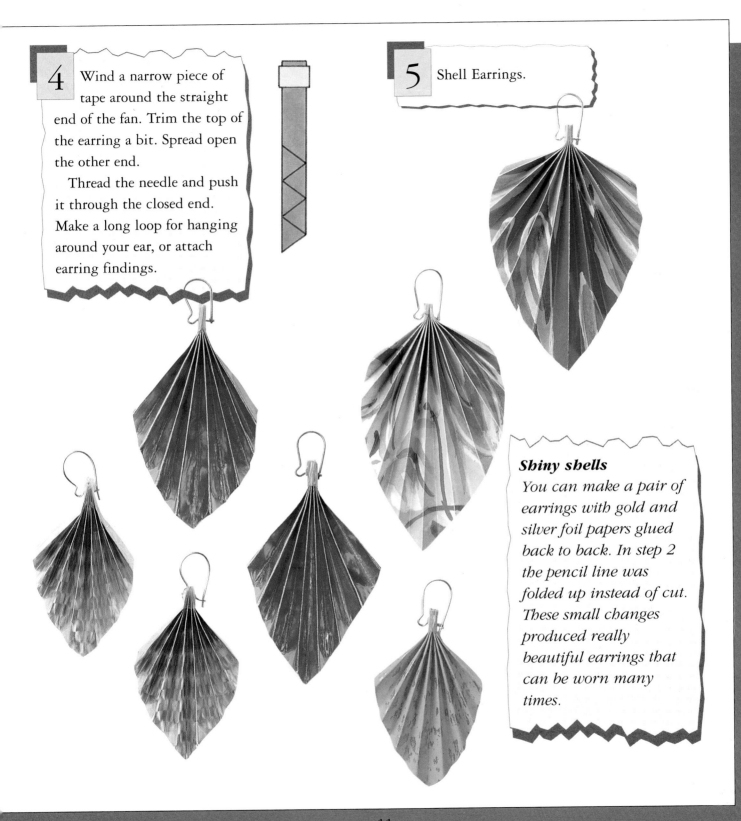

4 Wind a narrow piece of tape around the straight end of the fan. Trim the top of the earring a bit. Spread open the other end.

Thread the needle and push it through the closed end. Make a long loop for hanging around your ear, or attach earring findings.

5 Shell Earrings.

Shiny shells

You can make a pair of earrings with gold and silver foil papers glued back to back. In step 2 the pencil line was folded up instead of cut. These small changes produced really beautiful earrings that can be worn many times.

PAPIER MÂCHÉ BRACELET

Nobody would guess that these bright bracelets were made from old newspaper or other scrap paper. It's a two-step operation: you make bracelets one day, let them dry overnight, and paint them the next day.

You will need
Newspaper
Masking tape
Small disposable bowl
or other container
White glue
Kitchen foil
Poster paints

1 Crush a full-size piece of newspaper into a sausage.

2 Form it tightly into a circle around the widest part of your hand and cut off any extra. Glue the ends together.

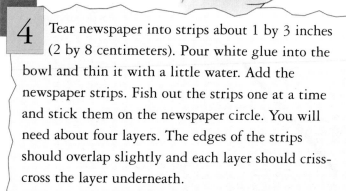

3 Wind a layer of masking tape firmly around the circle.

4 Tear newspaper into strips about 1 by 3 inches (2 by 8 centimeters). Pour white glue into the bowl and thin it with a little water. Add the newspaper strips. Fish out the strips one at a time and stick them on the newspaper circle. You will need about four layers. The edges of the strips should overlap slightly and each layer should criss-cross the layer underneath.

Set the bracelet on a piece of kitchen foil and let it dry in a warm place overnight.

5 Paint the bracelet with poster paint. Begin with a basic coat in a light color. After it has dried, paint on lines, wiggles, and circles with other colors. If poster paints do not stay on, use latex or acrylic paints, but be very careful not to spill any. Wash off any drips with water immediately.

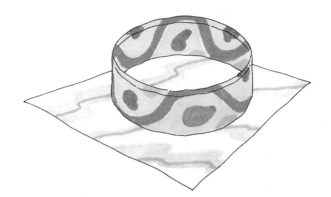

6 Papier Mâché Bracelet.

Friends together

It's fun to make bracelets with friends. You may want to substitute wallpaper paste for glue. It works just as well, but is a lot cheaper. When the bracelets are finished, you can glue on any kind of decoration.

CHRISTMAS EARRINGS

Little red boots hanging from your ears say that you are ready for the holidays. It doesn't matter whether you call them Christmas stockings or Santa's boots. You only need to cut two small paper squares and fold them like origami. To produce the contrast between the white fur cuff and the red boots you need paper that is red on the front and white on the back. Look for giftwrap or origami squares.

You will need
Two red paper squares with 2-inch (5-centimeter) sides
Needle and thread or earring findings

1 Place the paper with the white side up. Fold it in half. Unfold it.

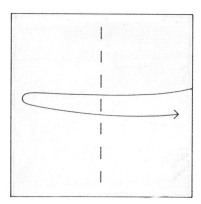

2 Mountain fold the top edge to the BACK. This will be the white fur cuff.

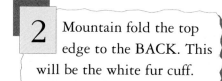
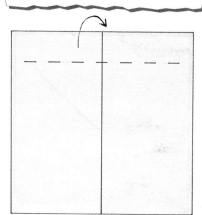

3 Draw a line from the left top corner to the bottom of the crease. Fold on the line.

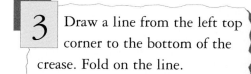
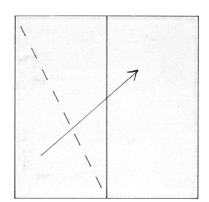

First tries

It's a good idea to learn the folding steps on bigger squares that are easier to handle. Try using squares with sides that are about 4 inches (10 centimeters) for your first tries. You can hang these boots on the Christmas tree.

4 Repeat step 3 on the right.

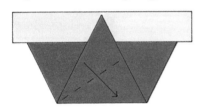

5 Turn the paper over to the red side.

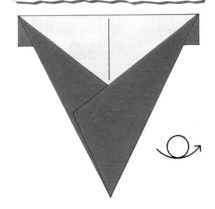

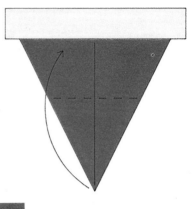

6 Fold the bottom corner to the top edge.

7 See the triangle on the front. Fold the left slanted edge to the bottom edge.

8 Unfold it.

9 Repeat steps 7 and 8 on the right.

10 Pinch the top of the triangle between your thumb and forefinger and push down to meet the creases you made before. See the next drawing.

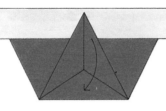

11 Roll the sides of the paper to the back and overlap them. Slide the top of the cuff under the overlap on the other side (or hold the cuff together with a dab of glue).

How to turn up the toe

When you have finished folding the boot, turn up the toe like this:

11A. Flatten the end of the toe, fold the tip to the back.

11B. Pull the tip up.

11C. Turned-up toe.

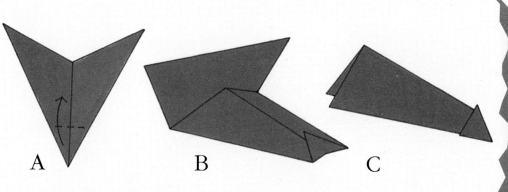

A   B   C

12 Pierce a hole on the left side of one boot and on the right side of the other boot. Slide on loops of thread or earring wires.

13 Christmas Earrings.

BEAD JEWELRY

Old magazines are a rich source of beads in all colors and sizes. It's hard to imagine that such beautiful necklaces and bracelets can be made from recycled paper strips rolled over a toothpick.
You can use almost any kind of paper to create a great variety of beads.
Bead jewelry makes wonderful gifts that your sister, your aunt, or other relatives can wear with pride. Your friends won't believe you made them yourself because they look as though they came from a professional crafter.

You will need
Colored paper
Ruler, pencil, scissors
Toothpick, long nail or knitting needle
Glue
Dental floss or yarn, wide-eyed needle

1 Cut paper into strips 8 by 1¼ inches (20 by 3 centimeters). Roll strips over a toothpick. Glue down end of strip. Hold bead until glue sets.

2 Pull out the toothpick. String the beads on dental floss. When the chain is as long as you want, knot the ends of the floss together.

3 Beaded Necklace.

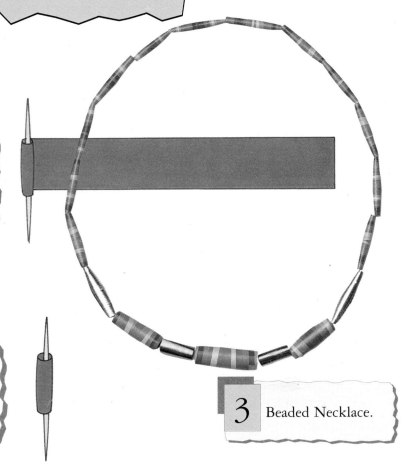

Tapered beads

Tapered beads are rolled just like barrel beads, but from long triangles. Begin rolling them at the wider end and roll evenly so that both sides taper evenly.

To make the triangles, cut a piece of paper 8 inches (20 centimeters) wide. At the top mark spaces 1 inch (2 centimeters) apart. At the bottom also mark spaces the same distance apart, but begin $\frac{1}{2}$ inch (1 centimeter) in from the edge. Connect the marks across the paper with pencil, then cut on the lines.

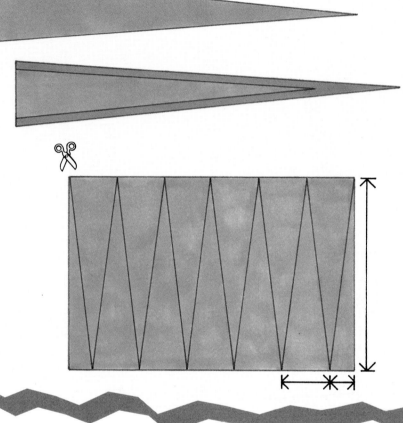

Paper

Almost any kind of paper can be turned into beads. Use thicker paper, like construction paper, to make bigger beads. Magazine pages and giftwrap result in multi-colored, thinner beads. Advertisement flyers can be turned into delicate pastel necklaces.

Spacers

You can separate beads with glass beads or pieces of straw. You can also hang on feathers, sequins, and other things.

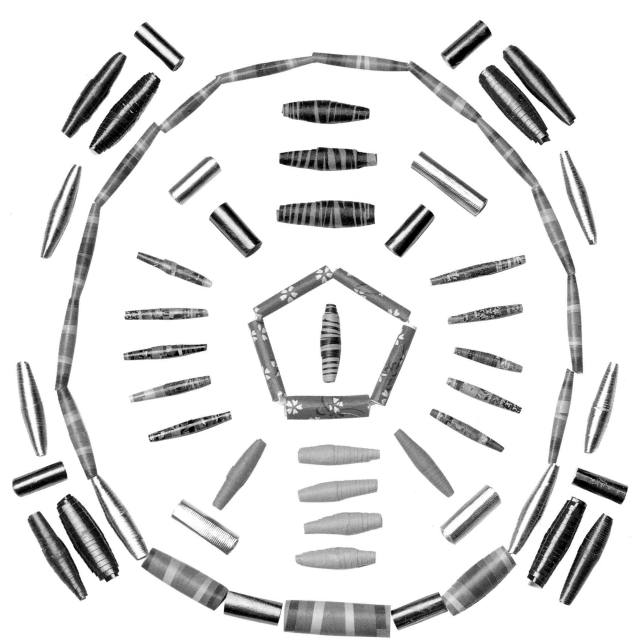

The bracelet is strung on a piece of thin rolled elastic to slide over the hand.

The brown and black beads are made from brown paper bags. Before rolling, a line was drawn with black marker near the slanted edges.

Other beads are made from magazine pages, giftwrap, origami paper, and metallic foil giftwrap.

ZIGZAG BRACELET AND RING

The zigzag pattern happens all by itself when you use giftwrap, shiny foil paper, or origami paper that is colored only on one side.

1 Cut the square from corner to corner. You will have two triangles. Each one makes a bracelet.

Two-color paper
You can choose two different colors for zigzag jewelry by gluing two pieces of colored paper together back to back.

2 Fan pleat each triangle back and forth, parallel to the longest edge. You should have a strip with four "ribs."

3 Roll it into a circle with the zigzag pattern on the outside. Push one pointed end into the opening at the opposite end. Hold the bracelet together inside with a drop of glue or sticky tape.

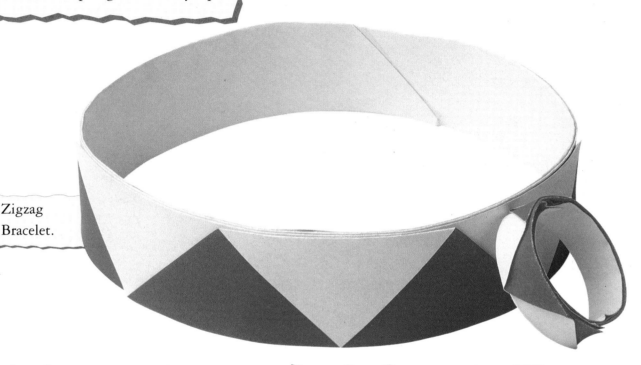

4 Zigzag Bracelet.

Pleating help

To fold even pleat lines, begin by making a halfway mark on the longest edge of the triangle. Fold the top corner to the mark. Fold the paper in half two more times. Unfold it flat. You will have seven creases that you can fold up and down in a fan pattern.

Zigzag Ring

Cut a square of paper with 2¹/₂-inch (6-centimeter) sides into two triangles. Fan pleat each triangle like the bracelet, but end up with only two ribs.

You can make the ring smaller or larger to fit the size of your finger by overlapping the ends a little more or a little less.

EGYPTIAN COLLAR

Thousands of years ago Egyptian artists created beautiful jewelry. This shiny collar could be in fashion today, but it imitates an ancient style.

You will need
Card, stiff paper, or thin cardboard
Metallic foil giftwrap in gold, green, and red
Ribbon, scissors, glue

Space age
Can you adapt the Egyptian Collar into something a space alien might wear?

1 Trace or copy the collar. Fold a piece of card in half. Place the outline of the collar on it, with its straight edge on the folded edge of the card. Cut out through all three layers.

strip

2 Cut slanted strips from all three colors of giftwrap. Glue them on the collar, overlapping them to follow the round shape of the collar.

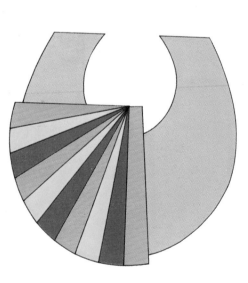

22

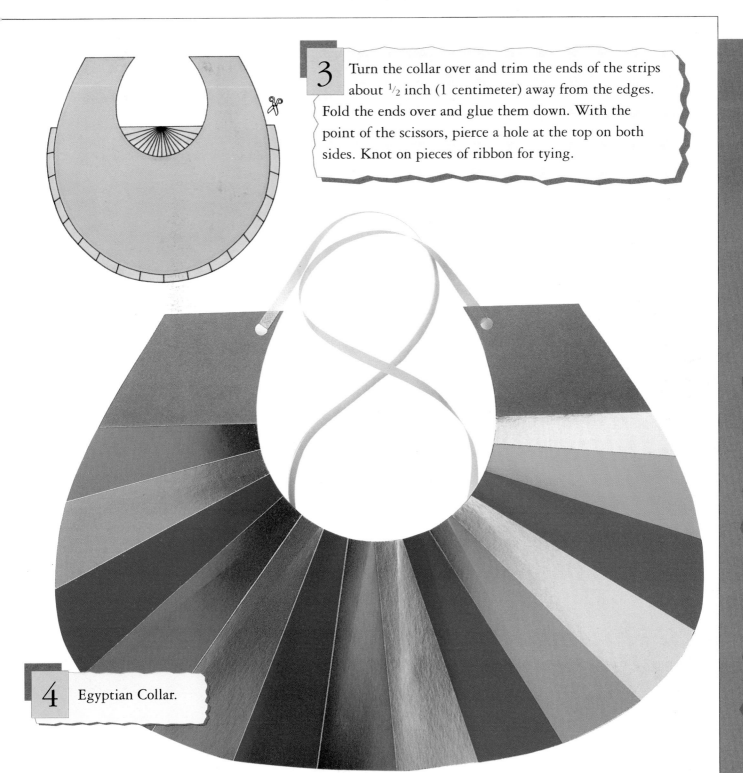

3 Turn the collar over and trim the ends of the strips about $\frac{1}{2}$ inch (1 centimeter) away from the edges. Fold the ends over and glue them down. With the point of the scissors, pierce a hole at the top on both sides. Knot on pieces of ribbon for tying.

4 Egyptian Collar.

DEEP SEA MOSAIC

The Romans used to decorate their floors with stone mosaics, but you can make a mosaic out of paper.

1 Cut out some plant shapes from the green paper, and stick them at the bottom of the blue paper. On the remaining blue paper, lightly draw with pencil some fish shapes and some wiggly lines for waves.

2 Cut your colored paper into small squares, roughly ½ by ½ inch (1 by 1 centimeter). They do not have to be perfect squares or all the same size.

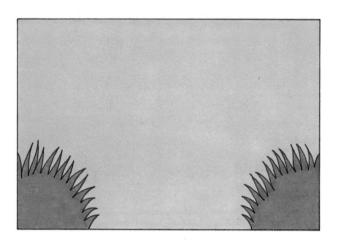

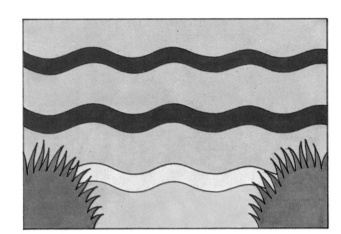

3 Select a color to use for your fish, and two colors to use for the water. Cover the blue background all over, but lightly, with glue. Start sticking the colored squares onto the background.

Trim some of the squares to different shapes, to fit with some of the difficult edges.

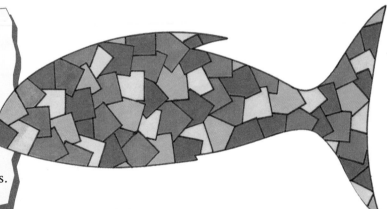

4 Deep Sea Mosaic.

STAINED GLASS FUN

A stained glass picture is easy to make, and looks wonderful with the sun shining through it. It makes a great present.

You will need
Black construction paper
Tissue paper in different colors
Pencil or light-colored crayon
Scissors, glue

1 Draw the outline of a tortoise on the black paper. Within the outline draw the head, two feet, and parts of the shell separately. Cut around the outline of the tortoise.

2 Draw around the black paper outline onto the tissue paper, then cut it out.

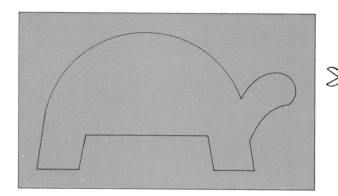

3 Cut out the shapes inside the black paper outline. Stick the tissue paper to the back of the tortoise. You can also add smaller pieces of tissue paper in as many colors as you like.

Helpful Hint
Cut out the shapes inside the outline by first piercing the paper with the point of your scissors, and cutting around the pencil line.

E.H.

You can make almost any picture into stained glass, but try simple ones at first.

CRAYON PAPER

You can make beautiful designs by melting crayons on white sheets of paper. Use crayon paper for giftwrapping, see-through window decorations, and for many other projects shown in this book.

You will need
White paper
Kitchen foil
A pencil sharpener
or knife
Crayons
Old newspaper
An iron

Caution:
Ask an adult to help you because you will be working with a warm iron.

1 Cover your work area with newspapers.
Put a piece of white paper on top of a piece of kitchen foil.

2 Pull the paper covering off the crayons. Shave slivers of crayons on the white paper using a pencil sharpener.

3 Place a second piece of foil on top.

4 Iron the sandwich with an iron set on low heat for half a minute. Remove both pieces of foil.

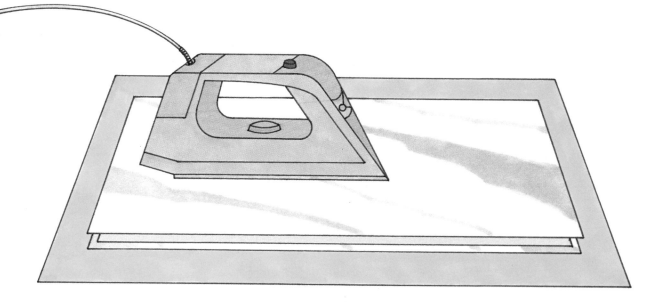

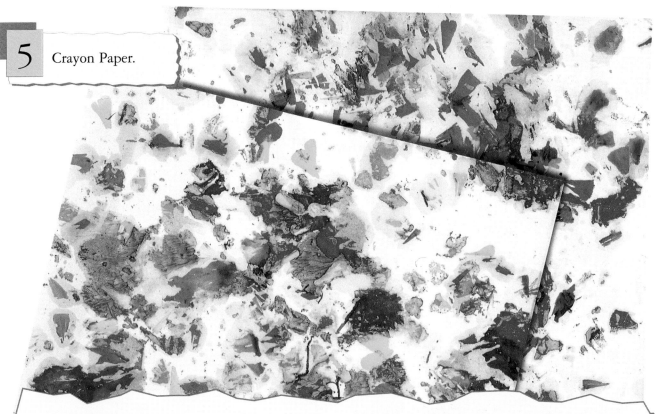

Giftwrap

Wrap small gifts with crayon paper. Wrap large gifts in newspaper or recycled shopping bags and decorate them with pieces of crayon paper.

Window See-Throughs

When you hang crayon paper in a window it will look like a piece of stained glass when the sun shines through it.

Suncatchers: *Draw circles, stars, flowers, butterflies, or any other shapes on pieces of paper with black marker. Shave crayons inside the outlines and iron them between kitchen foil. Cut out the shapes.*

Window Flowers: *Place dried flowers or dried leaves in the middle of a piece of paper. Shave crayon around them and iron them between kitchen foil.*

Streamers: *Glue or staple curling ribbon to the bottom of suncatchers and window flowers.*

Cover it: *You can cover See-Throughs with clear self-stick plastic sheeting.*

On the window: *Stick suncatchers or window flowers to the glass with tiny pieces of sticky tape. You can also attach a loop of ribbon to the top for hanging.*

TREASURE BOX

You can never have too many boxes. With paper you can make them in all sizes and colors, always ready for packaging a gift. But boxes have many other uses. They help you keep things neat and organized and you can give a box made from beautiful giftwrap as a present.

You will need
A paper square
Scissors

1 If the paper is colored on one side only, begin with the white side up.
Fold the square in half in both directions. Unfold the paper flat each time.

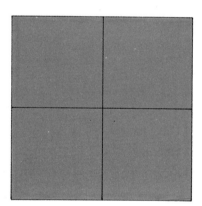

2 Fold each of the four edges to the middle crease. Unfold the paper flat each time.

Box with a lid
For a lid, begin with a square of paper ¼ inch (.5 centimeter) larger.

Basket
Staple a strip of paper to two sides of the box for a handle.

Bigger or smaller boxes
Begin with bigger or smaller squares. Make large and small boxes and put all sorts of gifts inside.

3 On a crease make cuts from the edge to the next crease, as marked with the thick lines.

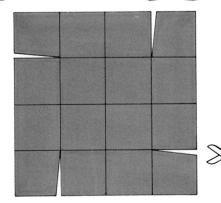

4 Fold the four edges to the nearest crease.

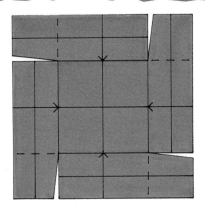

5 Crease sharply on the dotted lines and stand the edges up at right angles to the bottom of the box.

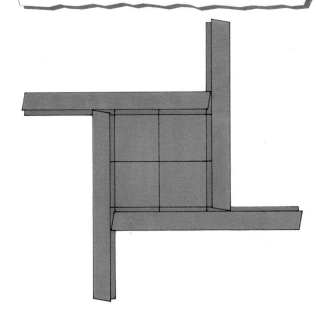

6 Fold the pieces that stick out (A) to the inside of the box.

Lift up the inside layer of paper at B and fold it over A. Lock in the other three corners in the same way.

The box will look better if you crease all four corners between your thumb and forefinger.

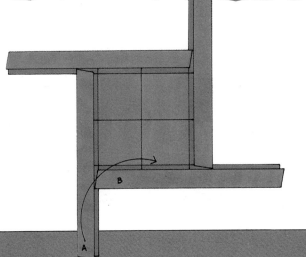

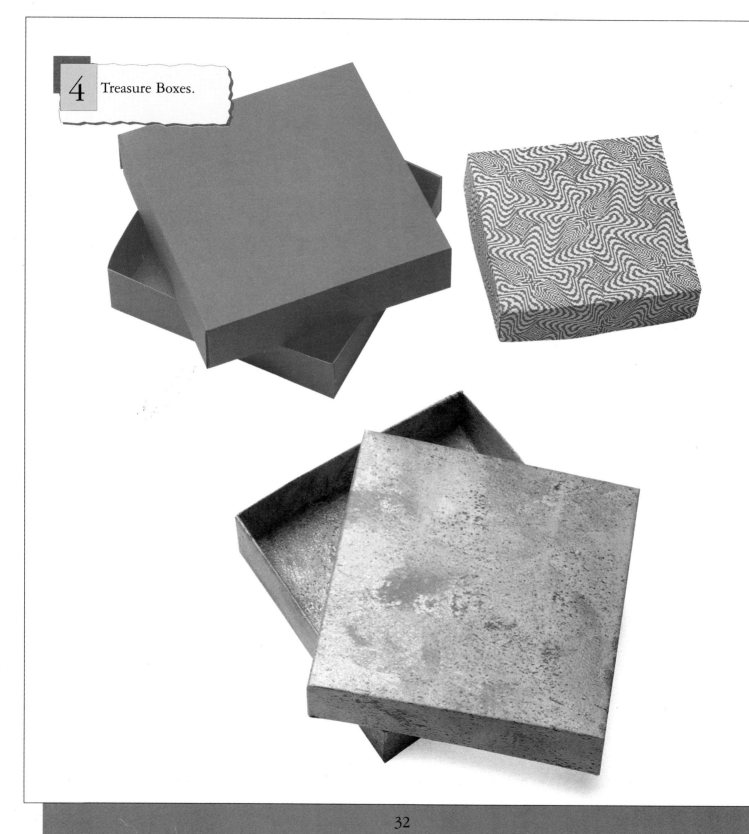

DIP-DYED GIFTWRAP

Once you have started dip-dyeing plain paper with gorgeous colors you'll want to keep on doing it. It's so simple and so much fun. You pleat a piece of paper and dip the corners into different dyes. You never know exactly what the sheet will look like after it is unfolded, but it's always beautiful. Use the paper for wrapping gifts, for bookmarks, and for ornaments.

You will need
White tissue paper (good quality)
Food coloring
Disposable cups
A bowl filled with water
Paper towels
Lots of newspaper to protect the working area and for drying dyed papers

1 For your first try use half a sheet of tissue paper. Fan pleat it into 2-inch (5-centimeter) wide strips.

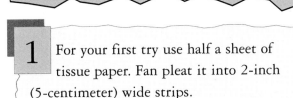

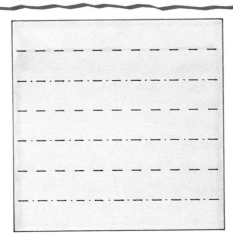

2 Pleat the folded strip again into a square bundle.

Careful
It's best to work at a kitchen counter near the sink. Cover the work area with newspaper. Wear old clothes and handle all dyes very carefully.

Rinse your fingers often in the bowl of water and dry them on paper towels. Otherwise, you may make ugly fingerprints on the dyed paper.

Triangle pleating
In step 2 fold the strip into triangles. Dip the corners as you did before.

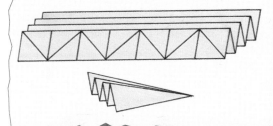

3 In a cup, mix red food coloring with a little water. Dip a corner of the bundle in the dye. Move it in and out quickly as you don't want to color the whole bundle.

4 Unfold the paper slowly, squeezing out extra water as you go along. Place the sheet on newspaper to dry.

Two or more colors

You can make red and yellow paper by dipping one corner of the folded bundle in red dye and another corner in yellow dye. You need separate cups of dye for each color.

Of course, you can use any colors you like or more than two colors.

Experiment

Try other ways of folding the paper before dipping, perhaps as a plane or an origami animal. Always dip one corner or one edge at a time, very quickly. Use full-size sheets of tissue paper or paper cut into flowers.

5 Dip-dyed Giftwrap.

HAWAIIAN QUILT CUTOUTS

Hawaiian women have sewn beautiful quilts for more than a century. The designs are based on tropical flowers and plants that grow in the Hawaiian Islands. Many square fabric blocks are combined and stitched together. Quilters create a paper design that looks like a snowflake. When they are really pleased with it, they transfer it to cotton fabrics.
They use bright colors that contrast with the background, but yellow and gold are traditionally reserved for royalty.
You can cut Hawaiian Quilt Cutouts from colored paper and glue them on gift packages or use them to decorate posters. The instructions include two full-size Hawaiian patterns you can copy.

You will need
Tracing paper
A square of colored paper
Pencil, scissors

1 Trace the pattern. Cut it out and set it aside.

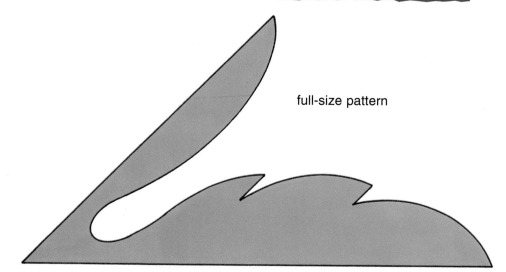

full-size pattern

2 Fold a square of colored paper in half…

3 …and in half again.

4 Fold the paper from corner to corner. Make sure you begin at the closed corner, which is the center of the paper.

5 Place the pattern on top of your paper triangle. Place the pointed corner of the pattern on the closed corner of the folded triangle. Draw around it and cut it out. Unfold the paper carefully.

closed corner

6 Hawaiian Quilt Cutouts.

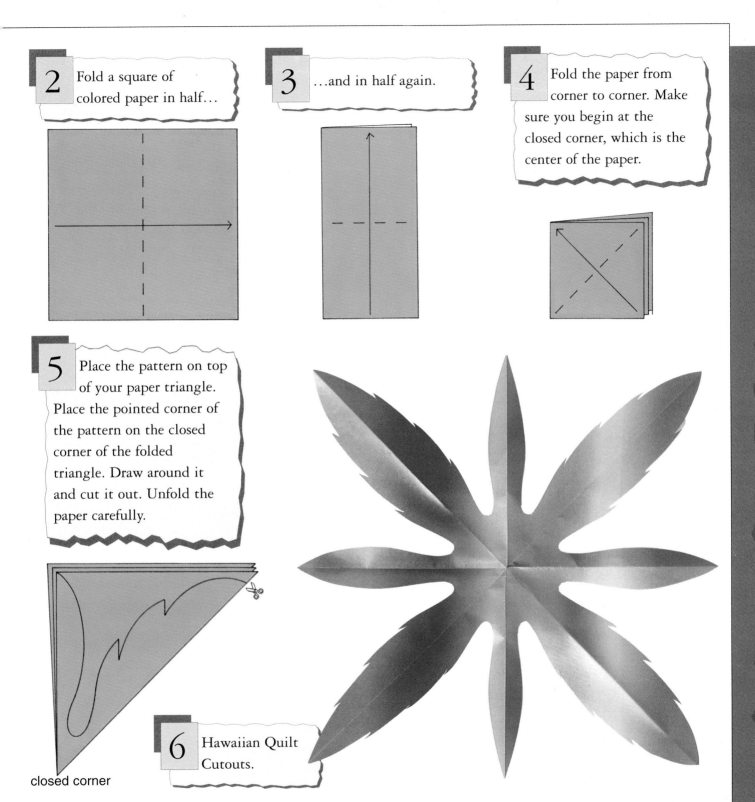

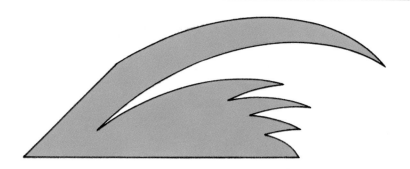

full-size pattern

POP-OPEN CALENDAR

How hard it is to wait for a birthday, the end of school, or another special occasion! Often children are given Advent calendars to help them count the twenty-four days before Christmas. Each day they open a window on the calendar and find a surprise. It may be a drawing or a tiny gift.

You can make a Pop-Open Calendar with windows that each reveal a surprise. It would be a nice gift for a friend or for someone in the hospital.

The instructions show how to make a calendar with seven windows, but your calendar could have twenty-four windows for an Advent calendar, or any other number you choose.

You will need
Two large sheets of paper, markers, pencil, ruler
Craft knife
Careful: *Craft knives are very sharp and must be handled carefully. Ask an adult to help you.*

1 On one sheet draw a picture of a Christmas tree, birthday cake, or plane (for someone going on a trip). Or you could glue on a picture or giftwrap.

2 With pencil and ruler draw on seven windows. Leave a wide margin on the four edges of the paper.

3 Cut open only three sides of each window with a craft knife. Bend the windows open on the fourth side.

Chocolate and other surprises.
Wouldn't it be even better if you could hide small gifts behind the windows? You can, if you create a space between the two pieces of paper. Glue narrow strips of thick corrugated card around the edges before you glue the two pieces together. Then you can tape a small toy, an origami, or a small piece of wrapped chocolate inside each window.

4 Glue the sheet with the windows on top of the plain sheet around the edges only. Fold open all the windows and draw on pictures that would interest your friend.
(A football, skates, earrings, a heart or anything at all.)

5 Close the windows and number them in the order they are to be opened.

PARTY MASK

Make a special mask for yourself or a friend. Wear it to a party. People used to dress up in fancy costumes and go to balls where they were disguised by their wonderfully decorated masks.

You will need

Stiff card, glue, sticky tape
Crêpe paper (or tissue paper)
Ribbon, scissors, giftwrap or
sticky stars to decorate
Piece of thin elastic or
a 1-foot (30-centimeter) rod

1 Trace or photocopy the mask shape. Put the tracing or photocopy on top of a piece of stiff, colored card or paper and cut through both layers. Cut the eye holes by using the point of a small pair of scissors to make the first hole, and then cut around the shape.

2 Cut strips of crêpe paper 4 inches (10 cm) wide. Gather and fold them to stick on the back of the mask, at the top, one on each side.

3 Make cut-out shapes from giftwrap, and collect sticky colored stars, felt-tips, or anything else that looks decorative and fun.

4 Take a piece of rod and decorate it by wrapping ribbon around it. Stick the rod to one corner of the mask using tape. Or, you can attach elastic to the mask and use this to keep it on your head. Cut a piece of elastic about 10 inches (25 centimeters) long. Make a small hole on each side of the mask, thread the elastic through, and tie knots in each end. You can shorten it if you need to.

5 Party Mask.

MORE GIFTS

When you have made some of the gifts and jewelry in this book, try experimenting with some of your own designs, colors, and patterns.

There are so many things you can create from colorful paper that make great presents for your friends and family.

In this book there are lots of projects for you to try, but you can think up even more for yourself. Look at the picture; it shows all sorts of things that you could try. Look in magazines and in shops, as well, for other ideas.

Be adventurous, and make magical paper gifts.